Goodb

Surviving Pet Loss, One Day at a Time

C.J. Protz

Carmel,
From my ♡ to yours,
thank you for everything!
You've taught me such
valuable lessons that
helped me on my grief healing
journey. You brought me Reese
+ Ryder ♡. Furever
grateful,
Carol 2025

A self-published title
Animal Dreaming Publishing
www.AnimalDreamingPublishing.com

GOODBYE, WALLY
SURVIVING PET LOSS, ONE DAY AT A TIME

A self-published book produced with the help and support of
Animal Dreaming Publishing
PO Box 672
Samford Village
QLD 4520
Australia

publish@animaldreamingpublishing.com
AnimalDreamingPublishing.com
@animaldreamingpublishing
@AnimalDreamingPublishing

First published in 2024

Copyright design © Animal Dreaming Publishing

Copyright text © C.J. Protz
cjprotz.com

A catalogue record for this publication
is available from the National Library
of Australia.

ISBN 978-0-6458836-7-1

Disclaimer
All information in this book is offered for educational purposes only. Please
consider and consult professionals in the relevant field to make an educated
decision as to whether suggestions in this book are right for you.

This book is dedicated to My Little Wally, for without you, this book would not exist.

I also dedicate this book to all the animal lovers throughout the world finding themselves making heartbreaking decisions and experiencing unbearable grief as they journey forward. I send my love as you endure your journey and as you eventually come through the other side of pain's grasp.

I see you. You are not alone.

Much love, C.J.

Acknowledgements

This was a tough, emotional book to write, edit and finish. Thank you to Sacha, Randy, Mom, Wendy, Brianna, Debbie, Donata, Carmel, Melissa, Tamara, Kelly Ann, Lissa, Tammy, Joanne, Sherri, Joy, Doreen and Nikki for your encouragement and support along the way.

Thank you to Scott and Trudy for the amazing opportunity to bring my book to life and for guiding me through the process. Thank you to Louise for her gentle, kind and effective editing skills. I am eternally grateful to you all.

The final thank you goes to My Little Wally for always showing up when I need his Spirit the most. May you live on forever in the words and emotions of this book. I am grateful for these memories that will last until we meet again.

♥

Invitation from Author

I invite you to open this book, open your mind, and open your heart. This book is in your hands right now for a reason. Explore why and enjoy the journey.

I've written this for you.

For you, the grieving, may my story help you heal and find hope for the future to laugh and smile. May you feel less alone in your grief. For you, the friends and family of the grieving, may my story help you to understand and become more compassionate to this type of devastating loss.

Contents

Introduction

Wally was the most amazing red, smooth-haired, handsome six-year-old male dachshund. He was given to me when he was only a year-and-a-half old. He arrived craving affection and attention and I was more than happy to give it to him.

Wally was an enormous, energetic presence wherever he was. He made me laugh constantly. He truly loved life. We would spend Saturday morning breakfasts together while the rest of my family and other dogs slept. Those times were quiet and we enjoyed being together. It felt special and connected. Come 7:30 pm, like clockwork, he would put himself to bed. He played hard and when he was tired, that was it. The off button hit.

He loved his backyard, and he loved being outside with me. He was my 'helper'. Any sticks I tossed away found their way to his mouth and the chase was on! He'd eventually drop them and continue running. With his butt down, he would zoom around the lawn as I chased him. He'd have a grin across his face the entire time.

A busy street is behind my fenced backyard and often the emergency vehicles speed past with their sirens blaring. Whenever Wally heard those sirens, he immediately raised his nose to the sky and howled for all to hear.

For some reason he hated plastic water bottles. The poor things didn't stand a chance against him. As a prank, I would leave a bit of water in them and when he went in for the kill, he sprayed water all over himself. Didn't ever stop him though!

Wally had one sister, a Pomeranian-Maltese named Molly, and a brother, a Chiweenie, named Dasher. Both were older than Wally. Dasher had the cutest ears. He could stand them up tall and he reminded me of Batman. I called him Batman every time he did that. Dasher was also quite the talker. He would use his voice to talk to me and he would get louder and louder if I wasn't paying attention. This would then turn into barking if I didn't listen. Dasher loved to play ball in the backyard – that is whenever Wally didn't steal it!

Molly put up with Wally, but she didn't really care about him. Wally picked on Molly all the time like a pest. One day Molly was standing in the kitchen. All of a sudden, Wally blasted in running at full speed. He completely ran into Molly like a bowling ball into the pins, sweeping her off her feet in a split second. Wally just laughed. You could just see the glee in his eyes! He repeated this a number of times. Like I said, he was a pest to Molly.

Dasher loved Wally. Even though Dasher was older it was as if he looked up to Wally as his older brother. Wally seemed more confident and stronger than Dasher so that may have been the reason.

Despite his comical antics, Wally did respect both Molly and Dasher. At feeding time he was very gentle and patient and ensured both of them ate before him. He was sweet!

Unfortunately, Wally had a very mean side to him. When the annual set of Christmas Villagers came out of their storage boxes for the season, I returned one day to find that mayhem and destruction had descended upon the Village! Trees were mowed down and snow was everywhere! The people figurines were lying strewn about as if a big monster had attacked them – and it had! Wally! I had to laugh. He acted so innocent – as if it couldn't have been him. Molly and Dasher were nowhere to be found implicating Wally alone.

I'm not really sure why he was mean at Christmas. My son was wrapping a present and Wally snuck in beside him and grabbed the roll of paper and ran! When he stopped, he placed one paw on the roll and with his teeth he began to shred the wrapping paper as fast as he could. He was absolutely entertaining. "What did that paper ever do to you Wally?" we said, laughing. In the end, we had to give him a snack to trade for the paper roll.

Wally was also an amazing actor – or so he thought. One day I went into the living room and there was a pillow that had the stuffing ripped out of it. The fuzz was everywhere. Wally came out walking nonchalantly as if he didn't do it. The one thing he forgot was the piece of fuzz sticking out the corner of his mouth. Busted! It was hilarious.

Anyone who has owned a dachshund knows the wiggle they have when they walk. It's a wiggle-strut walk that is the cutest thing to watch. Every walk I smiled as I watched his happy wiggle. Dachshunds often exhibit human characteristics and Wally was no exception. I would be in the kitchen doing something and Wally would sit on a nearby sofa. He sat at the edge and placed his front leg and paw on the arm of it. He would sit and watch and keep me company. I loved it.

I took Wally everywhere I could. He came on road trips with me and I always felt protected. I was never lonely when he was around. Wally had no boundaries when it came to privacy. He would follow me up the stairs to be with me, wait for me to come out of my shower, join me in the washroom, and pretty much anywhere he could find me.

Wally had a way of making everyone feel loved and special. If a guest of mine was at the door to leave the house, he would sit directly on their feet as if to say, "Don't go, stay." He always received extra pets when he did that as well as a lot of "Awwwww" words and love from the person. He was sweet and lovable. Anyone who met Wally, loved Wally. They truly did. Wally had the softest smoothest fur that added to everyone's petting pleasure.

He was also a very trusty confidante and companion. I confided in him constantly and it seemed like he understood me. He would give me kisses on particularly tough days. He knew what I needed.

In 2013, my marriage to Randy broke down and I moved to a city five hours away with my son, Sacha, and my dogs Wally, Molly and Dasher. I was now closer to my parents and my sister and her family, even though they were still an hour's drive away. I continued to work from home and didn't meet many people. My friends were back in Sherwood Park. It was a lonely time. Wally sensed my sadness and loneliness and he stayed next to me at all times. I would often hug him hard – I called him my living teddy bear. I expressed my feelings to him, and he would kiss me. He was my confidante – my safe place to vent, the only one I could vent to.

Wally adored me and I adored Wally. He brought love, joy and laughter into my life every day and I honestly thought we would have many, many years to go.

After Christmas in 2013, I had the idea of moving back to Sherwood Park. I talked it over with Randy and we agreed to live separate lives but physically in our home together to be there for Sacha at all times. Watching Randy and Sacha's teary goodbyes during our year away was heart wrenching for me as well as them. We returned to Sherwood Park once school finished in the summer of 2014.

Unfortunately, that decision didn't sit well with many family members or friends. How can you live together like that? They thought it was a terrible idea. Who does that? They couldn't understand my reasoning. I knew I needed to do it for my son and my soul. Having been apart a year made it easier to do as well.

This decision strained many close relationships to the point of losing them altogether. I couldn't understand – I was the same friend I had always been. Nothing in me had changed. I would have respected them if the tables were turned. It hurt.

I continued to work from home and focused on raising my son and dogs.

In 2015 I decided I would try new things and meet other people as life became very isolated. I chose to attend a women's empowerment class. It was a short 10-minute drive to the country to a place called River Lane Ranch. The scenery was beautiful. It was peaceful and serene, a wonderful escape. The host, Carmel Joy Baird, was very welcoming and a very interesting lady. She was a psychic medium and taught other classes, including this women's class. I'll never forget what she said to me on that first night. "If you continue to come here, it will change your life."

I thought, hmm, okay. I'll see. She was so right as time went on. I met many amazing ladies at these classes. I eventually began attending psychic development classes and expanded my circle of friends. I had found my tribe in both. My Spirit loved their Spirits. It was safe to be myself and speak openly about my life and experiences.

My circle of friends was changing, and I was feeling happier. My son was happier and doing really well in school. He was back with his old friends. My dogs had their favourite backyard and home again too. I felt optimistic about the future.

On March 12, 2016, Wally woke up and his back legs were paralyzed. He was diagnosed with Intervertebral Disc Disease (IVDD) and needed surgery for any hope to walk again. In the days that followed, I would visit him at the hospital and practice the rehab exercises on his feet. Finally, six days later on March 18, I was able to bring Wally home. He had been very grumpy and "bitey" with the staff and they thought Wally returning home might make him feel better and lift his spirits.

Wally yelped as I put him into my truck. We got going and he 'spoke' to me the entire trip home. I think he was telling me what he thought about it all! He was not happy.

Dasher was so happy to see him, wagging his tail and kissing Wally. It melted my heart.

Molly walked by and as if to say, "humpff, who cares?"

I settled him into his pen and massaged him a bit. He tried to nap but he appeared to be having back spasms of some kind.

Later that day, I got him ready with the leash and sling to take him out for a pee but he wouldn't move. I went to remove the leash off his neck and he yelped loudly before I had even touched him. I went to try again and he tried to bite me. That broke my heart. That wasn't like my Wally at all.

Wally began yelping more and more. I prayed he would heal quickly and that his pain would subside. The sounds he was making were heart-wrenching and nerve-wracking. It made me emotional. I prayed I could handle this.

It wasn't until early the next day that he finally let me walk him with the sling to the patio door. He stepped outside onto the deck – just one step – no more. He put his head back and closed his eyes as the sun shone down on him and he sniffed and sniffed. His nose was just-a-going! It was a beautiful day. It was a beautiful moment to witness and share with him. He finished and looked up at me. He looked the healthiest at that precise moment; more than he had looked for a long while. He wanted to return inside. He went back into his pen.

As the day progressed, Wally was in so much pain. I spoke to the vet and became fearful. It wasn't good. If I couldn't get his pain managed, I would have to let him go and that broke my heart. Wally began shivering. His pain medicine should have taken effect by now, but it hadn't seemed to. I petted his head and he yelped. As long as Wally didn't move, he looked more comfortable. He rested his head on my cushion. He looked at me with a 'look' in his eyes that I didn't want to acknowledge. He wanted his pain to end.

The downward slide began. He kept crying and yelping and I was full of sorrow. Whenever he tried to sit he was in so much pain. He would look straight at me each time he tried to rest. I sat and looked into those eyes as they pleaded for the pain to stop. And then I knew. That moment outdoors ... he wanted one more sniff of the backyard. He wanted to be home again one last time to see Molly and Dasher and us. He knew ... his eyes said it all. And he wanted me to help him. I didn't think my heart could break anymore, but it did. It broke more and more as the night went on.

We put a blanket around him and loaded him into the truck. I drove. Randy held Wally tight. I rolled the windows down in the truck so Wally could get more sniffs in. Every time he moved, he cried. I jumped every time. My nerves were shot. Inside the hospital the vet checked Wally's toes and sure enough Wally had no feeling whatsoever. Chances were he had another injured disc and the prognosis wasn't good.

It was devastating news. I had to make a decision. My tears began to flow. I had to let him go. It was the toughest decision of my life.

As I've come to know, many people are judgmental about grieving the loss of a pet.

"He's just a dog," they said.

If only people understood how hurtful that matter-of-fact comment is to someone grieving such a deep loss.

Or, they'd say after a time, "You should be over it by now."

I would ask, "What is 'it'?"

I pray that some of these people read this book to understand how devastating pet loss can truly be. With great love, comes great loss, regardless of who it is. The ache is so deep. I miss touching him, hearing him, cuddling him, playing with him and being with him.

I've since learned over the years that there are holistic options that may have helped Wally. Acupuncture, prolonged crate rest and physiotherapy are a few. If I could go back in time, I would definitely try those options before surgery. But we only know what we have available to us at the time.

Heavy sigh. If only …

I love you Wally ♥

Part 1

Heartbreak

March 19, 2016

"His heart has stopped."

The doctor's voice seems to come from far away.

I hold Wally tightly to my heart, telling him I love him. "I'm so, so sorry, Wally." Tears fall as I stroke the smooth fur on his face and forehead. I'm not aware of the exact moment of his passing. My grief is too extreme. I can only focus on his face and on petting him.

The vet says I can stay as long as I need to.

We sit together like this for a while, with Wally close to my broken heart. My shattered heart. This is my boy, my *baby*, and my best friend.

Still sobbing, I tell Wally a lot of things:

"You have to find a way to come through to me – tell me you're okay."

"When I die, I want to see you first! You have to greet me!"

"Find my dad and my grandmas."

"This wasn't the way it was supposed to be!"

I am grief-stricken and mad. Why? Why My Little Wally? My happy, joyful Wally?

I finally have to leave. I need to go before his body turns cold beneath my fingertips. I also need to leave while I can still walk, and not fall to my knees in anguish.

Randy walks over to me and hugs me. I sob and sob. The pain is unbearable. "Where's his blanket?" I ask the staff. They bring it from the back and tell me it is soiled. Feeling annoyed by that comment, I say, "I don't care. It was part of him. I can wash it at home."

I will clean it and care for it forever – it will always be symbolic to me.

Randy drives me home. When we arrive, I barely get the words out to my son Sacha through my tears. He hugs me, and soon he is sobbing too.

I can't believe it. Is this even real? My aching chest tells me it is. I email Mom and my sister right away, despite it being 1:30 a.m. I can't bear to hear them ask, "How's Wally?"

I just can't.

My son, Dasher, and I sleep together that night. I clutch Wally's collar in one hand, and his second blanket – an unsoiled one – in the other as it had Wally's scent. I place the blanket between us. My son and I hug it as we try to go to sleep.

March 20, 2016

I wake with a splitting headache, a sore back and a broken heart. I barely slept. I get up. I feel numb. I put on my "hugging sweater," as I call it. Wally loved sleeping on it and in it whenever I took it off. I had been wearing it when he passed in my arms. His scent lingers.

I open the email from my sister, Wendy, on my phone. Her words bring me to loving tears.

"I am so, so sorry, Carol. My heart breaks for you. I know I can't do anything to ease your pain but know that you are all in my thoughts. Wally had a wonderful life with you – you gave him a second chance at a real life. I hope he will shine through from the other side, and his memories will fill your heart. I will miss him dearly."

"Thank you from the bottom of my broken heart. He truly was my best friend. I feel broken." I reply.

"I have been in that broken place too, and a part of you will always be broken – with that kind of connection it never goes away. The days and months ahead are going to be the loneliest and saddest, but in time it will ease. Take some time for you now. If you need anything at all, let me know," she writes.

I call my mom. She's read my email. "I don't know if I should tell you this," she says. "Last night I dreamt Wally had died."

"I'm so happy to hear that, Mom! Wally crossed over. He's okay. He got that message to me through your dream. Thank you so much for telling me."

My reaction surprises her. Hearing about her dream gives me so much comfort.

During the day I do a variety of things: laundry, look at pictures of Wally and reply to caring texts or posts from friends on my Facebook page. It all brings me to tears. In between, I think of Wally memories and cry. I'm full of guilt, sadness, and pain. You name it, I'm feeling it.

Dasher does not leave my side. He is with me constantly. It's very unusual for him to behave this way. I think to myself, I bet Wally talked to him and asked him to take care of me when he was gone. Later, when I talk to Wendy, she suggests Wally was likely at my side all day and Dasher sensed his Spirit. I cry. My sister cries.

Wally was so young and full of life when he died: the biggest personality! My house is so quiet without his energy. He *was* the house. He *filled* the house. He also filled my life and filled my heart. My heart was a big furry heart thanks to him.

I have to make decisions about what to do with Wally's body. While talking to Mom and my sister, I figure out a perfect plan. I would cremate Wally and put his ashes into a special dachshund -shaped pendant to keep him near my heart every day, even though he was in it already. I also had four special places to take his ashes:

1. The tier in my backyard. He loved running up those raised areas in my yard! This way he could always enjoy the space, watch over it, and be with me outside.

2. My sister's walking trails. Wally loved her and their walks together at her acreage. I will give her some ashes so she may walk his path in privacy and spread them along the way to say her final goodbye.

3. The special "Digging Tree" at my parents' farm. He once thought he had a mouse under that tree. It was a hot summer day and he dug and dug. His sweat mixed with the dirt creating a muddy mixture that rolled down his face. It was really comical. The mouse had escaped, but Wally had no idea. I think the mouse was even laughing – from many trees away!

4. The beach. I had always wanted to take Wally to the beach and watch him playing in the sand and waves. Regrettably that never happened. I would pick my favourite beach. Ironically, I'd already made plans to go to that beach and would be there on Wally's birthday of July 22.

I sit outside enjoying the sunshine and heat, remembering Wally. I think about him doing his favourite things – about him not doing them any longer. Running, chasing, chewing water bottles – always putting in one hundred and ten per cent!

It is only a few hours since I'd lost him, and my day is so tough.

The tears keep flowing. I think to myself, how do I have so many tears?

I crawl into bed, a bed so quiet, so empty without my Wally. I miss his cuddles. I finally get up and grab Dasher to cuddle. I clutch

Wally's collar and blanket – inhaling deeply for a whiff of him before drifting off to sleep.

March 21, 2016

I awake smiling, feeling joyous and grateful. Wally had visited me in a dream! It was the best gift ever – the one I truly needed. He told me he loved me and was happy. Wally was okay! The decisions I had made were the best ones for him, he told me.

I cry as I retell this story to family and friends, receiving a lot of "yays" and "wows" from them all.

I now want to document as much as possible about my special Wally. Tonight, as I write, the tears still flow but I know My Little Wally is happy on the other side.

I back up my photos on my phone today. I have some real gems! I even have a video of him killing that roll of wrapping paper at Christmas. So hilarious and so him.

That makes me smile.

As I finish writing, Dasher is lying next to my leg and under my arm. I'm scratching and massaging him and am grateful to have him here. The house is quiet, but my Wally memories are loud and boisterous and mine for whenever I need them.

I miss your physical touch and your personality, Wally. I hope that once my grief lessens, I can raise up my energy and be able to sense your Spirit and continue our relationship.

I love you, Wally.

March 22, 2016

I receive a beautiful email from my sister, Wendy, with such touching and profound words.

"I hope you have a better day tomorrow, Carol. You need to take one day at a time, then two, then it's going to be a month, and then it's Christmas, without Wally. It's going to be a long, hard road but you'll make it. I did. When I lost my dog it was absolutely devastating for me. She was my everything. She was with me 24/7 and we did everything together.

"She was by my side every step I took, with every ride in the truck, every night in bed, and I spent more time and talked more to her than any one person. My heart and soul were empty when I lost her. It took me many, many days and months before I felt a little bit better. But you never forget or get over it with that kind of connection. It gets a little bit easier. I still remember every detail, every wonderful moment with her, and the sad, sad morning she left us. I will never forget her.

"I was fortunate when my next dog came into my life. He and I too shared an amazing connection – and I so needed him in my life. The day I lost him killed me inside too. Yet another piece of my heart died that day. But I scraped through, day by lonely day. And to this day, I remember everything about him, both the good and the sad times. I thought I would see him, hear him, and at times I could feel him after he was gone.

"Not all connections are like this; not all dogs are like this. Your Wally was. You had that connection with him, and it was amazing. He needed you as you needed him. And it's unfair and you both needed more time together. It's so, so unfair and I don't understand why this can or should happen when you love them so much. But it is what it is. It's tough and you're breaking inside, but it will get easier with time.

"I wish I could ease the pain you're feeling right now but I know there's nothing I can do to help you. 'Time' is the only answer. I do hope with Carmel's help and with the support of your friends, your healing will be quicker. I'm sure their support and knowledge of the other side will bring some peace to you. Look at Wally's pictures, talk to him if you need to, and go through your memories over and over again. He will always be there for you."

Wow. Wendy's message is so beautiful and poignant. I relate to her heartache. Why did I have to lose Wally? I hadn't told anyone yet, but I'd written books and had planned Wally and I would travel to book signings together and have the best time ever. But it was now just a dream.

I remember that somewhere in the last few days I had received a whispered message, "You have another book to write." I know this means a grief-related one, and I want to run as fast as possible to get away from that idea.

I grab my "hugging sweater" and hold it tight, inhaling as deeply as possible to catch a scent of my Wally instead.

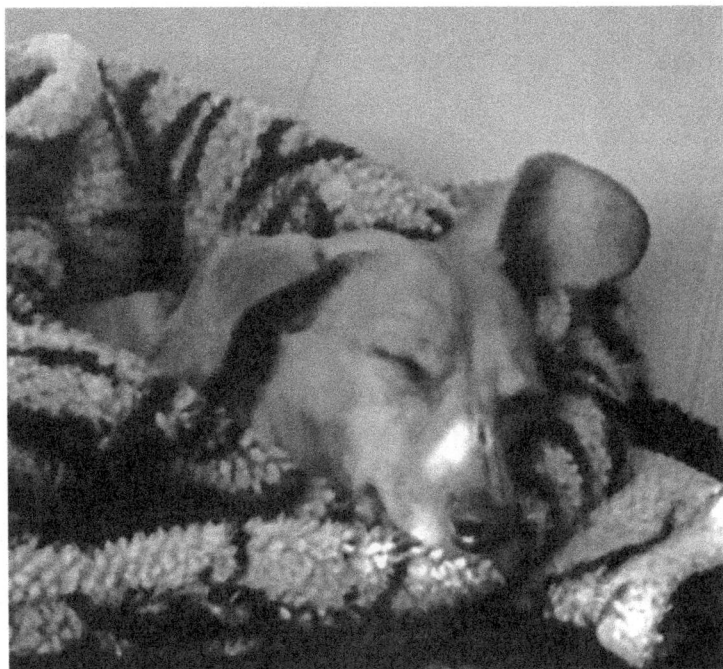

March 23, 2016

I feel so much anxiety about returning to the vet hospital to discuss Wally's cremation and to complete the paperwork today. When I arrive, they give me Wally's fur clippings and paw prints that were done the night of his passing. His fur is redder than I thought it would be. What an odd thought to have, I thought to myself!

While I'm grateful I don't have to sit and wait in the reception area, they put me in the exact same room he passed away in! How can they do this to me? Don't they realize what room this is? This is where My Little Wally died in my arms! I'm trying not to cry as I wait for the technician to come in. She walks in and begins to tell me about my options for Wally's body. Part of me is in disbelief that this is even happening but the other part of me knows the devastating truth of reality. Tears stream down my cheeks as I nod and listen.

I finally tell her I want him cremated. I want a specific urn with the personalization of "My Little Wally" on the outside. I also want some ashes in a pouch that I can spread outside. It feels so final. "It is final," I think to myself. More tears fall. A part of me wants to rush to the back-room cooler right then and there and grab him and hug him to make sure this is actually real.

It bothers me so much thinking of him in that cold back room all alone.

When I leave, I feel like I'm abandoning him. I speak out loud to Wally all the way home. The talking makes me feel good! The sun is shining. Sunny days were his favourite thing.

When I return home, I receive a message that my photos are ready to pick up. Yay! I leave straight away. There are many pictures of Wally, including some of he and I together. They bring immense comfort to me. I place them all around my desk. One picture in particular stands out. He is lying on his sofa in my office looking at me. This one feels really good to look at, so I place it front and centre. It's like he's still at work with me.

The lady at the photo centre had said there was no internet traffic at all today for some reason, so she thought she'd print my photos early and get them to me today. A small miracle.

Thank you, Wally.

March 26, 2016

A week ago today I lost my Wally. I continue to feel so broken-hearted – heartbreak and guilt all wrapped into one. I miss him so much my heart physically aches.

Despite my anguish, Wally has tried to show me his Spirit is here with me. This morning there were dog pawprints in the snow in my backyard, along the path that he always walked. Molly and Dasher never venture on that path – not ever! I know in my heart it was a sign from him to me. And of course, how timely as the sun melted it quickly. I'm glad I'd taken a photo.

I've also seen a flash of Wally's eyes in Dasher's eyes. A superfast flash but I know those eyes. Speaking of Dasher, all of a sudden while we were in my backyard, he grabs a rope toy and whips it around! This is definitely more of a Wally move than a Dasher move. Either Wally's playing or Dasher's wanting to make me feel better.

I won't lie. Today is really hard. I pray that God will resurrect Wally tomorrow on Easter Sunday! For me, please? That will end my pain – my suffering in silence.

I feel so empty – so angry. Why? I trust God and the Angels, but … if I didn't have and want to be here for my son, God could take me too and end this pain! At least I'd be with Wally.

My house is too quiet. I miss the:

- 🐾 "Ruh ruh roo" in welcome. Wally would "speak" with that sound. The tone would change at times depending on the situation. Sometimes it was happy sounding and other times it was like a tattling-on-Dasher tone.

- 🐾 Tormenting Molly. "I love to tease you, Molly!" was Wally's ultimate goal – always! (sorry, Molly, but I do miss it!)

- 🐾 Barking.

- 🐾 Running past me at warp speed.

- 🐾 Greeting as I step out of the shower.

- 🐾 Pushing the door open to visit me in the bathroom.

Now? The empty toilet paper rolls just lie on the floor. You don't come in and steal them to get chased thinking you've outsmarted me!

So many memories. So much love. Such a huge, epic loss. I am lost without you.

I venture out to my local greenhouse today. Walking amongst the living plants helps my energy a bit. Nature truly has a way of healing. I buy an etched stone that reads, "If love could have saved you, you would have lived forever." It is absolutely perfect for how I feel.

When I return home, I place the dachshund statue urn in front of the fireplace; a spot Wally loved to be in cold weather. From the side, the urn looks so much like Wally. I put the stone and an Angel next to it. It's currently warm weather so the fireplace is not being used and I can safely create this little memorial for Wally here. It gives me comfort. "You have your Angel wings now, my beloved Wally. You always did. You saved me and loved me more than I've ever experienced. I cannot wait to see you again."

All week I have felt devastated, incredibly sad, heartbroken, unsure of how to go on, powerless over this loss. I need to change this in order to move forward.

❀ I am thankful for loving Wally all the years that I had him until his very last breath.

❀ I am thankful I held him as he crossed from my life to Spirit.

❀ I am full of love for My Little Wally.

As I think about you, Wally, I couldn't be more amazed by how much you lived life! Despite what had to be an aching body, you gave so much to everything you did. You were up for anything – everything was an adventure to you. You ran everywhere as if to make the most of your time here. You loved me so much and I felt your love all the time – more than I've ever felt in my entire life. You were always happy and smiling and talking. Your "ruh ruh roo" was beautiful to my ears. You had so much gusto!

I didn't realize it then, but you taught us all so much about being happy. All this while you likely hurt and felt tired from your aging and degenerating back. While I know now there were a few signs that something was changing – they were so subtle that I never would have noticed except while scanning all my memories after your passing. You weren't acting "poor me", "why me", "moping", "pouting" – none of that! You embraced life with more gusto and passion than anyone I've ever known. You, My Little Wally, are an inspiration to me. I am so grateful you came into my life. I wish it could have continued forever, but I have to trust God. You have a permanent loving home in my heart, mind and Spirit.

I love you, Wally.

Part 2

Feathers

March 28, 2016

I'm sitting at my desk in my home office, missing you, Wally. You always slept in here. I could stop work and place your soft face into my hands and give you a cuddle. Your face was as soft as downy feathers. I'd know you were always here. Now, when I look at pictures of you in the space you occupied, it aches. If only a miracle delivered you into my arms right now. I miss you so very much. I cry with hurt and sadness.

God I loved you, My Little Wally. Except for my family, I don't think anyone realizes the depth of my pain. Suffering in silence, surviving moment to moment, and trying to be a functioning parent to my son. This is my daily life.

I open my email and see I have my weekly "Signs & Symbols" course from Carmel. I've been a student of Carmel's since 2015 and it's been very amazing. Spirit has really opened my eyes and awareness.

This week's message tells me to watch for feathers as a sign from my loved ones on the other side. Immediately I think of Wally. Placing my right hand over my heart, I take a deep breath and tell Wally he needs to show me feathers – really show me feathers – to let me know he's around. This is an intense, heartfelt request. With my hand on my heart, I take some deep breaths and release the request.

And so it will be.

March 29, 2016

Can't sleep. As I lay there thinking, I realize how wicked my ego has been during my grief. I realize I've been edging God out. Telling myself so many negative things: "you should have", "you could have", and "what if?" Relentless to a point where I'm at the edge of Grief Canyon ready to fall in so deep I may not be able to crawl back out! Right then I tell my ego to back off and slam it with all my positives and love for the situation. I take my control back. My ego has been quiet for the most part ever since. BGB (Bring God Back) is the opposite to how I'd been behaving.

I immediately feel love and know My Little Wally is with God, sitting on his knee at times, running and chasing birds and bugs and creating laughter and havoc, as he did so well when he was here. I envision this moment when God looks down at Wally and asks him, "Did you just lift your leg on my robes, Wally?" and Wally smiles. Then God says, "You little … Right. I did create you, didn't I?" and his booming laughter ripples through the skies.

Wally would do that. The image in my mind makes me laugh.

I'm registered to attend psychic development class tonight. All day long I ask Wally to show himself to me somehow. On the drive to class, I ask Wally again. As I walk into class, I ask Wally again. Class is uneventful … until the end.

I walk up to Donata, the instructor, and she gives me a hug. She looks out the window and says, "Look who showed up!" It is the peacock that lives at the Ranch. At that moment, I didn't think anything of it.

I am finishing something when I overhear Donata telling Brenda, a lady in the class, something about the peacock. I ask, "What did you say that peacock's name was?" Together they say, "It's Walter!"

After being noticed, Walter turns around to go home.

Mission accomplished!

The floodgate opens. Donata and Brenda look at me and their eyes fill with tears also. We all hug knowing this is a message from my Wally (Walter). I explain how I'd asked him to show up somehow. It is such a beautiful moment that words do not begin to give it justice. One of the ladies tells me that Walter the Peacock had never come to the house in the eight years she had been there. He was usually afraid to venture too far away from his own home.

By now my classmates are wondering what is happening. I know this is a safe space. The group are very kind when I share about Wally's passing.

My classmates hug me, cry, and tell me stories about their own dog losses. It is a very moving experience. Everyone is supportive and caring, and I felt like everything will be okay. A lady tells me that Wally and I must have had a very strong bond for him to do this. She says that Walter was prancing around, trying to get attention, "Look at me! Why aren't you looking at me?" as he went from window to window.

This was just like Wally. He was always doing things that say, "Look at me!"

I thank Wally on my drive home for delivering such a beautiful message. You did a great job, Wally!

March 30, 2016

I actually slept seven hours! I was so happy and full of peace thinking about the peacock.

I have a much more settled day, feeling Wally in my heart.

This evening, I attend another class out at the Ranch with my women's group, a different group than last night, but the same instructor, Donata. Guess who shows up? Yes, Walter! The instructor laughs, puts her hands on her hips and tells me, "Carol, can you please go visit your dog!"

Walter stands on the deck and I watch him. He begins performing, jumping to another window and standing on a ledge, garnishing more attention from the ladies inside as well. He's peeking in the window as if he's trying to see someone ... me! He really wants attention! It's really funny – and it's a behaviour so typical of my Wally. I go to the window to look at Walter. I smile as I look into his eyes. He flies down to the ground and away. Turning back to the group, I tell the ladies, "Okay, I can go home now, I've seen my Wally!" and we all laugh.

Donata explains to the group what happened the night before. One of the ladies from the office, Tamara, pops in and says Walter had not been at the Ranch all day. She's heard about the visit last night. When she sees Walter outside tonight, she turns to her colleague and says, "Carol must be here!"

My Wally has come through again.

Every time that I see the peacock now, I smile and know he's become my Walter – for me and to all those ladies who witnessed it in the groups. A happy moment I will cherish always. As one lady said, I can have a relationship with Wally on the other side now. It's different but it's still very similar.

April 1, 2016

I sit outside after work today, watching so many birds fly to my feeders. Dasher chases them on and off. Dasher explores the same path Wally always did, and lifts his leg on the big rock too! I think Dasher can smell Wally and follows the scent. Dasher has always had exceptional ability with scents.

Then I realize. This week my symbol and signs to watch for are feathers. I hadn't thought much about "live" feathers and was expecting to see those on the ground. Well ... look at my week's events! Peacock Walter – twice! Birds, birds, and more birds in my backyard – unlike anything before.

I say, "Wally, you did good, my love!"

April 5, 2016

I get these little moments of extreme sadness, yet they still surprise me. I told Wally on my drive yesterday that I need to let go of the "final moments" memory as it haunts and saddens me profoundly. I ache at times with the loss. I miss Wally so very much.

My symbol to watch for this week is pets and how they act and react around me. It feels ironic that I get that word "pets" – now, of all times. Why now? It both saddens and angers me to hear this word when Wally is missing from my life.

I cry many tears today as I re-read the emails after Wally's passing. They are tough, emotional and raw.

Tonight, the vet hospital calls to tell me Wally's ashes are in. I'll go in the morning. My son briefly thinks that you are back when I tell him you are ready to be picked up at the vet.

I wish it were true.

April 6, 2016

I drop my son off at school and go to collect Wally's ashes. I handle the visit better than I think I will – it is a quick exchange. I return home and unpack the urn and Wally's ashes. When I read the card, the tears flow. The big, loving personality is reduced to such a small urn. Reduced, but a huge Spirit lingers in my heart, my home, my world.

I feel some peace having Wally home with me now.

I collect my mail. I get another sympathy card for Wally and I cry some more. There are also some pictures of Wally from my sister. They make me smile.

Knowing how blue I feel, I believe what happens next is Wally's doing.

I am in the kitchen and Dasher is with me. I look down. Dasher looks at me with his right front paw in the air as he stands. He never does that. This is something Wally always did. I say, "Dasher! You never do that, what's up?" Dasher puts his foot down and lifts the left front paw instead. Again, another Wally move.

Remember the message to watch for signs from pets for the week? Voila!

Wally. It was unmistakably Wally.

April 8, 2016

I am creating a memory album to honour Wally. It is a scrapbook filled with photos and stories that express how I feel about him. I have his inked paw prints in there as well as his fur clippings. I want to capture every memory I can. I hope it helps to lessen my grief.

I went to a memory album class at Brenda's home tonight instead of going to another class at the Ranch – her dog did not leave me alone. He loves me. Was this another message about pets for me to notice? I love his attention knowing what was going on. Wink, wink. Brenda takes him upstairs after a while because he keeps on distracting me.

As I drive home, I talk to Wally about the evening. I speak to Wally while driving all the time now. It's comforting.

I'm doing okay with my grief. I'm owning the pain and feeling all of it. I'm also openly admitting it's tough instead of saying "It's fine."

April 9, 2016

Dasher warms my heart with another Wally move. He waits at the door to the basement. I open it and he goes down first – on his own. He never does that, but Wally always did. When Wally was tired, he headed straight down to bed. I smile at Dasher and say, "Hi Wally!" The coolness of the basement is ideal for sleeping and I used to sleep down there with Wally. Sometimes Dasher would join us, but it was always Wally who lay next to me. Upon waking the next morning, Wally's head would be on the pillow with his face directly facing mine. I loved that!

April 10, 2016

Shattered into surrender. These words sum up the weeks following Wally's passing. I can't bring myself to say Wally's death. It's too harsh, too final. I clean and move things around today to keep busy.

I miss Wally. But if I start dwelling on the memories, the sore opens too wide and I bleed pain. I worry I'll forget him, though, and that really bothers me. I want to learn to connect with him on the other side even more.

Tonight, Dasher sits at the door to the basement and barks. He has never done that! Maybe someone was egging him on?

April 13, 2016

I've been grumpy and angry for the past few days – so fed up with this grief. Women's group is on tonight. I debate with myself all day on whether to attend. No signs either way, so I go. I'm so glad I do! Walter presents himself in fine style again – peeking in on us from the window, getting our attention, and then flying to the upstairs balcony.

Before I came to the Ranch, I'd asked Wally to show himself again. We had a new teacher tonight and she had heard about my Wally experience, but this was her first time bearing witness.

All the ladies look at me and smile when Walter shows up.

I walk to the window to see Walter. When I return to my seat, I say, "Okay. Now I can go home – I've had my Wally medicine."

Everyone laughs.

April 14, 2016

Wally visited in a dream. This time he came with a family message to cheer us up. Wally slowly walked to our front door, tail wagging and joyful. "Whenever you enter the house, bend down and pat me. I'm right here waiting for you!" Just thinking about this makes me feel a bit better all day.

I go for a massage because my physical body aches throughout. It mirrors the ache of not having your touch, Wally. It really does.

April 16, 2016

Tough day. I did yard work, but this time my Wally wasn't here to help me physically. I'm sure he is here spiritually. There are plenty of sticks he can play with and chew, plenty of sirens on the highway he can howl at, plenty of sunshine he can bask in and enjoy, and many dogs next door he can talk to. Dasher is with me but he's a different personality type. Dasher's more like a little baby to take care of.

I bought myself a peacock solar light for outside. A friend had told me where to get one. Every glance at it reminds me of Wally and how much I love him.

I cry a lot, tonight. The ache doesn't leave. I miss Wally's touch and personality. I miss the intimacy I felt with him. He may have been a dog, but he felt like my soul mate.

April 17, 2016

I gently bury Wally's ashes under the peacock. Tears quietly trickle down my face. I spread a few ashes along the fence where he would visit with the neighbour's dogs through the cracks in the weathered boards. I smile and cry at the same time. I'm touched by the memories. I've put the remainder of his ashes aside for other locations.

I sit quietly. I feel very alone. Sometimes it feels like my heart will shatter if I think of you too much. I sure miss you, Wally.

Later on that evening, Dasher acts like he is channelling Wally again! He chases a water bottle, rips off its paper, chases it and fetches it to me … okay, that bit's not Wally. Wally would have destroyed it in seconds! But it's still not typical Dasher behaviour whatsoever.

As I lie in bed, the emptiness creeps back in like a heavy, hurtful fog, seeping into every crack in my heart. Will the hurt ever ease up?

I love you, Wally. Good night.

April 18, 2016

I had another Wally dream visit! I had asked him to come because I was having trouble sleeping and felt an overwhelming sadness for him. He was standing on something very high up in the air.

"Wally! Don't jump! You'll get hurt!" I yelled.

He jumped down, bounced up from the ground right into my arms for a huge hug! "I can't get hurt," he said.

It was the best hug I could ever ask for.

I got up and let Dasher into the backyard. When I open the door, I can't believe my eyes. "Oh my God." I say to myself, out loud.

In the middle of my lawn sits the largest male mallard duck I have ever seen. His head is such a beautiful, brilliant green. Dasher soon notices him and barks and runs toward him. The duck flies straight up and heads east. Just then a female duck flies out from the trees in my tiered area of the backyard! Talk about feather signs galore! I had never had a duck in my back yard, and now there'd been two.

April 19, 2016

One month ago, to the date, Wally died. Every moment I wish I'd wake up and it wasn't real. Some days I feel like I cannot go on. Having Sacha to think about gets me through the dark moments. I try to practise gratitude, but it's hard to do right now.

I am thankful for the love I had with you, Wally, and I would do anything to have you back. The pain is incredible. The loss is devastating. My tears flow. Huge drops hitting these pages. A tear-stained letter to us.

Dasher. What a character. I watch him through the window. He comes to the patio door. There he stands, prouder than anything, with Wally's large, dirty bone in his mouth. He wants to bring it inside. "No way Dasher, that's yucky!" I laugh. I take a photograph of Dasher through the window just as I had done with Wally with that same bone, all the while wondering if Wally has led Dasher to it somehow?

Molly hasn't been feeling very well these past few months. She had surgery in February to remove crystals from her bladder. Molly sleeps a lot and doesn't interact with us much. I don't even want to think there could be something more serious going on.

Not now, please God. Not now.

April 20, 2016

Dasher is outside as sirens blare on the street behind the house. Dasher howls! Dasher never howls! Four times with nose to the sky, he howls for all to hear, kicking up grass the whole time. It's such a Wally move.

April 23, 2016

The moment of time that hovers just before waking is a special moment. Wally appears, standing next to my loveseat. He puts two paws on it and jumps up beside me without any effort. I smile, then, poof, I'm awake!

Thank you, Wally. I needed to see you.

I sit down to enjoy a Saturday morning coffee, without Wally. How wrong is that statement? I look at your urn and photo and question why … I guess I'll never know until it's my turn to cross over. As I head off to an art class, I ask Wally to show up somehow today.

As I work on my class project, the teacher comes up to me. I look up and to my left – I laugh inside – I see the shape of her head and hair and the warmness of her smile. Over my painting, it somehow looks like a photo bombing that Wally would do.

I had just met this lady today, the teacher, and had told her she looks familiar. Of course! She reminds me of Wally! But I can't tell her that!

While all this goes through my mind, she asks me if I have a wiener dog. I am surprised until she points to my ring. I nod, and she tells me about having one growing up and how much she loved her dog.

She understands when I tell her I lost Wally a month ago.

April 25, 2016

I am extremely emotional today. I sob and sob for Wally. I feel so blue. I don't feel well either, I have a headache and queasy tummy. It's raining and raining, adding more gloom to the day. Somewhere during the day, I read something that sounds like it could result in potential grief relief:

- ❀ Write your pet a letter.

- ❀ Write down all the feelings you have.

- ❀ Once done, rip it into pieces and bury it, releasing all of those feelings.

It's worth a shot, I think. Maybe I will try.

April 26, 2016

I think Wally visited me in my sleep, but I can't fully recall. I wake with a sense he'd been there. Some days I worry so much that I will forget too many details about Wally. It bothers me immensely.

April 27, 2016

Dasher runs up the stairs into my office, fast. He steps onto a basket to get closer to me, tail wagging and incredibly happy to see me. As I look into his eyes, I swear I see a flash of Wally looking back at me. This makes my heart swell.

A short while later, I speak with Randy about Wally and begin to cry. Randy leaves the house and only minutes later he texts me that he has seen a dachshund going on a walk near my home. This is no coincidence! I feel some peace and calm.

I sit outside in the sunshine after lunch. I write Wally a letter. I sob the whole time. When I finally finish, I rip it into tiny pieces and bury it with tears. I tell him I love him over and over. I know Wally loved me and would never want me feeling so badly. I think the process helps me. I tell Wally I need to feel better and raise my vibration in order to connect with him. I also tell him I will truly honour his Spirit by finishing this book and his memory album. It is a goal for me, too, something to work toward.

I register last minute to go to women's group at the Ranch. I hadn't been sure about going, but decide it would be good to get out. It is good and I feel better being around the ladies.

I'm disappointed that I didn't see Walter the Peacock tonight.

It's a bit later than usual when I return home. Dasher is excited to see me. His greeting is the same as it used to be from Wally. Dasher has taken over Wally's role as greeter.

An hour later, when I am laying in bed almost asleep, I stir and wake. I feel something different. Dasher has crept in and is asleep at my head. I sense a warm pressure alongside my knee and hear a tail thumping on the bed, ever so gently. I know who it is immediately. I keep my eyes closed so I don't break the spell. After a while, I sit up, but no one is there.

It was Wally. I'm sure. The feeling was absolutely wonderful.

I realize this has happened because of the release of emotions with the letter. My desire to move forward with a Love and Light vibration instead of the painful vibration allowed the connection.

April 28, 2016

I think I hit my rock bottom of grief yesterday when I had my huge ugly cry with the letter. I feel like I am starting to climb out of that slippery pit. I know I'm going to slip and fall, but I finally see the cliff's edge above, especially when the sun shines. Sunshine is my medicine of choice. Maybe it's because Wally loved it too.

April 29, 2016

I attend a group event with a medium. It's about an hour away from home. Some family members are there, so I'm not feeling alone. There are about 20 people altogether.

At these events, messages given to others often resonate with me too. The group is connected and present together, so it's bound to happen. Many of the messages are things I've learned, but the reminders are welcome. Some key ones are:

- ❧ Be in sunshine.

- ❧ Colours are important – wear colour – be around colour.

- ❧ If you've lost dogs, know they are perfect!

- ❧ Put crystals under your bed for sleeping. (I use a rose quartz that night and have a decent sleep.)

- ❧ Lots of messages come up about writing books for kids, but not to me specifically.

One message directly to me is most peculiar yet accurate. The medium asks me if I find dogs. I reply I do. She says I have a way with them, and that I could be working with dogs and animals somehow in the future.

As I write this, I recall a message I received during one of my meditations and want to capture it in case I forget! Wally clearly told me that feathers were definitely "our symbol".

May 1, 2016

I pat the spot near my pillow as I prepare to sleep. I ask Wally to come. Seconds later I feel a cool breath like a kiss on my nose. It lasts awhile – over and over.

Thank you, Wally.

May 2, 2016

I feel very frustrated at my job. The small petty issues anger me, more so than usual. "Who cares!" I feel like yelling, when they complain about the most trivial things. My heart is aching so much in silence.

Maybe it's time for a change.

May 5, 2016

I am angry and impatient with everything lately. I'm having a hard time at work. It all seems useless and unfulfilling. What's the point.

I miss my Wally.

I reach out for help, today. I can't shake the grief. I don't want to take meds to numb the pain. In a few days I will go for a healing with Eagle Healing. It is with an Indigenous Elder, Doreen and her granddaughter, Sherri. They believe pets are family members.

They hold no judgment about my grief. I'm really looking forward to it. I've thought of going for a long time. Who knows, maybe I will even be able to enter the Spirit World during the session and visit Wally myself! I know in my heart I need this. My world is very grey without Wally, and I thrive on colour. I need it back.

I'm feeling quite annoyed and disappointed. Many of my friends, outside of my women's group, don't bother to ask how I am anymore. When you lose a pet, the same sympathies or understanding doesn't seem to exist. It angers me greatly and makes me miss my Wally that much more. I always had him to talk to, to confide in, and then snuggle with.

May 6, 2016

Last night I cried myself to sleep. The heartache was too much to bear. It's now morning. Some close to me think that I'm pushing myself to get over you, Wally, by going to the healer. I feel stuck in everything I do right now. It's like a paralysis of Spirit. I see no one unless I go to women's group. I've only had one visitor since Wally passed. How sad is that? I feel alone and invisible. Wally filled such a void in my life.

May 7, 2016

I am nudged to contact a fellow classmate, Joanne. Joanne had told me that I had a furry heart when we did an exercise with cords of energy in one of our previous classes. I call her and it turns out she owns a dachshund. She said that when she told me about the "furry heart" she heard "Best dog mom ever" and saw a glimpse of her own dog. We both believe Wally came through to say that. That was the same night the Walter the Peacock story began as well. Her words brought me such comfort, and I shared that with her. I can't wait to meet her doxie now. The nudge to call her seems like it was Divine and perfect timing.

May 8, 2016

Today is Mother's Day. It's early and quiet. I hate the quiet without Wally. These early morning moments were always special with him. He and I together equalled contentment. I open my email. Nothing interesting. I open my Facebook page and the first post I read is a photo of a brown long-hair dachshund wishing doxie moms a Happy Mother's Day. Perfect.

Thank you, Wally!

May 10, 2016

Had a rough sleep. I am grateful when morning arrives. "Wally, today is healing day!"

I wake up Dasher. He isn't ready to get up at 6:30 a.m. and is still fast asleep! I open Facebook. A white moose symbol is the first post I see! The white moose symbol is one I use with my dad's Spirit; he'd passed many years prior. I share the picture to keep it for myself. "Thanks Dad," I say. I am comforted that everything will be okay today, and that he is here.

I drive to the nearby city and find the address I need. I am early and have time to get a snack and write while waiting. I have a slight headache today. As the time nears, I pray. "Wally, I truly want to see you during this healing session. Truly. I love you and I want to feel better. That's why I'm here. I need to rid myself of the painful traumatic memories of your passing. I want to release that extreme pain to the Light. I want to focus on joyous memories instead. My love for you will never change and my connection with you on the other side will be stronger than ever. I will see and feel you as my vibration will be higher. I also wish to release the job I have for what my soul needs and trust it will provide in abundant ways I can't even imagine. No limits."

I love you, Wally.

I go to the healing session. Sherri greets me at the door of her home with a warm, inviting and smiling face. Doreen is there as well and also welcomes me warmly. I feel very comfortable and at ease instantly. We enter the basement to begin. The three of us stand and prayers are made to the Four Directions as we move simultaneously to those directions.

The healing begins by tuning into the Spirits around me. Wally is there. Elder Doreen describes him as a show-off with short legs. "Look at me," he says. There is a message about blankets. I smile, knowing the significance. Given a chance, Wally would chew holes in blankets constantly!

"He doesn't like you being sad," the Elder says. "When you experience him, his Spirit, you are happy. He doesn't want you thinking of him suffering at the end. Think happy, joyous memories."

The granddaughter says Wally and I had saved each other. I tell her I always say that, as does my sister.

"You healed Wally. You are a healer. What made you connect to Wally?" the granddaughter, Sherri asks.

"He was alone and needed love," I say, softly.

"That's what you needed. That's how you saved each other." Sherri speaks of family and how I miss them. "Wally wants you to spend more time together."

"We've spoken more since he passed," I say.

"He's doing that," Sherri says. "What did you like in Wally?"

"So much! His joy for life, being happy, always having fun – all the things I want to be!"

"Exactly! That's what he showed you – why he showed you. You needed him," the granddaughter says.

"Your little guy is running all over. Little partner," the Elder says.

I tell them how I always call him My Little Wally.

The granddaughter says Wally and I were placed in each other's paths on purpose – he only left earlier. She says that when the sad thoughts come in to switch to happy memories of Wally. To get into that habit.

"That will get rid of the boo boos. Listen to my granddaughter – God is working through her to help you, so listen!" the Elder says.

The Elder then talks about other health issues, for example, she knew I had headaches, and also relays messages from family members who had passed away. It is wonderful. The Elder then says, "You have a teenage son. He is sad right now because you are. This healing session will make you both feel better."

That hits me hard. I can see it myself with my son.

I lay on my back and close my eyes.

The granddaughter feels my stomach. "I can feel the cords in there. Stuff needs to come out."

Tendon-like strands run vertically across my middle. I had never noticed those before. Both ladies work on me to release everything. Once finished, my tummy feels soft. It is amazing.

They tell me to relax again.

"You are seeing the colour green now, " says the Elder.

"Yes! How do you know?"

"I see what you see."

I relax even further … and I see Wally! He is looking at me laughing and smiling as we walk. "Look at what I can do now," he tells me, jumping and carrying on. I see rocks and shells – we're at the beach in my vision.

"I always walk with you," Wally says lovingly.

A bit later, a chill descends over my arms and chest. At the same time, the granddaughter says she can see feathers around me. I know it's a hug from Wally. I really feel his love.

Next is some smudging with a feather to refill my heart after what was lost.

"The two of you used to look into each other's eyes – a lot. Really look. You always had such intense eye contact. This is important to relay to you," says the Elder.

This was exactly how Wally and I communicated. Often without words, looking into each other's eyes, we spoke and understood each other. As I thought of this, an image of myself as a child having fun pops into my head. It was Little Carol reminding me to smile and yes, be happy!

My session is over. Together, the three of us worked on removing my burden of grief. I feel lighter and grateful for everything that transpired during my session. And, I almost forgot, Wally says, "It's okay to love another dog."

It was a physical, emotional, mental, spiritual healing all in one. I feel lighter. I go home, then I pick Sacha up from school. I tell him about my session. He tells me I look happier.

May 11, 2016

I need to take back control of my life. I need to meditate and pray on what I need to make that happen. I go for a walk with Dasher, but he is scared and cannot wait to return home. At lunch I sit outside to meditate, with my feet on the grass. Dasher jumps up on my knee. My phone rings before I can start. Wally's pawprint is ready. In a quick 50 minutes I have the pawprint in hand. I pray I never have to set foot in the vet hospital ever again. I'm amazed how much that one phone call and trip back into the city lowered my mood today.

I remind myself to be gentle with myself when this happens.

The pawprint looks nice. His pads are heart shaped. I gently out-line the indentations of his paw print with my fingertips. It's good to have Wally home now – all the parts of him. I sit outside again, noticing there are a lot of these little pod things all over the grass. I pick one up. It is shaped like Angel wings. So bizarre yet so very cool.

I say thank you, Wally.

Part 3

The Girls

May 14, 2016

I don't think I will actively look to own another dachshund, but if one needed a home like Wally had needed one, I will consider that.

May 16, 2016

I have a voicemail asking me to call the Ranch as they have a question for me.

In my mind, I hear, "Ryder needs a home."

I call. Ryder is a dachshund and she does need a home – as does Reese. They are a bonded pair and need to be together. I say I would give an answer the next day.

But the decision is already made.

May 17, 2016

"I will take them," I say when I call. They are pleased and not surprised. My son and I arrive at the Ranch in the afternoon to pick up the girls. I had met Ryder before but had never seen Reese. Both are beautiful mini dachshunds with exquisite colouring, very different to Wally's red. Upon closer inspection, I see Ryder has a distinctive marking on the top of her head between her ears. It is greyish white in colour. It is a similar shape to that of a peacock feather! I say to myself, "Of course it's that shape."

As we walk to the truck, who should be standing next to the truck looking inside? Yes, Walter the Peacock! So funny! I am glad my son witnesses the peacock overseeing this event. Now Sacha understands what I've been telling him because he saw it firsthand. This makes it more real. As we drive home, my son begins to cry. He hadn't realized how much he missed Wally until he saw these dachshunds.

This ended up being a fast and powerful manifestation from May 14. I am positive Wally has had something to do with it.

Now I have four dogs at home.

May 19, 2016

Ryder has Wally's eyes. When she looks into mine, my heart melts. I see my Wally in there. She also has the same three whiskers and a similar, brown-coloured nose. She chooses me right away as her person. She is my girl, my shadow. First night home she sleeps under my armpit. She is really tiny compared to Wally. She makes the odd low-sounding growl and it sounds like Wally.

Reese kisses a lot, explores, plays and is more vocal. The girls wrestle. They jump off Wally's couch onto their bed and onto each other. It's hilarious! Dasher takes to Reese first and they play and chase each other. Dasher doesn't stop smiling! He has playmates! Molly doesn't care the girls are here and pretty much ignores them. I enjoy the girls, but it is bittersweet. I still miss Wally, even more because Ryder reminds me of him.

Today is Ryder's second birthday. It is also two months to the date of when Wally passed. It seems ironic how I have two mini dachshunds here today. Ryder is about the age that Wally was when I took him in also.

Thank you, Wally.

May 21, 2016

Sacha, the dogs and I travel to the farm. We stop to pick up a few groceries. As I come out of the store, a huge raven lands on the back of my truck! I am amazed at how large it is. Another feathered message! That has never happened before either.

May 23, 2016

I take Wally's ashes to his special Digging Tree. I sprinkle some of his ashes on the Digging Tree, the other trees, the pasture and the garden; everywhere that we walked around here in the past. I know you are with me, Wally.

A robin appears as I finish.

Feathers.

Thank you, Wally.

May 30, 2016

The week at the farm was good for my Spirit. Being away from the hustle and bustle of the city and work was a welcome escape. All the extra time outdoors in wide open spaces and bright blue skies was like medicine for me. Walking through Wally's favourite spaces made me smile. The girls had an absolute blast playing at the farm and their youthful energy was fun to watch. Many bouts of laughter were caused by those two.

With vacation over and work commitments waiting for me, I'm back at home. I step into my home office and once again realize my office assistant, Wally, isn't here.

I'm having a very tough day today. Missing Wally so much. I want him here next to me so badly. A wave of emptiness, sadness and longing sweeps over me. I try all the tools I know of to overcome the feelings, but I'm human and I falter. The frustration at work has amplified my grief.

Wally filled such a void. Even the girls don't fill that one. Intuitively I don't know what to do. I am blocked.

June 1, 2016

I attend my class wind-up tonight. Walter the Peacock stands on the fence as I drive in. I say, "Hi Wally!"

Carmel asks me if Ryder has chosen me and I say yes. Smiling, she says she thought so. Carmel says the day before she called me to get the girls, she had been in her reading room when Walter the Peacock had flown up to her window. He was continually pecking at the window; something he never did. She had told the office staff and they said that Walter only does that when Carol is here. Carmel then realized the message was about me.

Carmel says Wally orchestrated the entire thing to get the girls to me. She tells me that when Ryder first came to the Ranch, Walter the Peacock played ball with Ryder, nudging it to her.

I feel energized after coming to the class.

June 8, 2016

I attend a webinar and some of the answers given to one lady really resonate with me, answering questions that have been on my mind a lot lately.

At the same time, a message pops into my mind, "Give her your spot at the June 26 class, she needs it."

I really want to attend this myself, but the message is insistent. I send a message to the class organizer to give this lady my spot. They reply straight away, telling me I'm wonderful. They also tell me they are converting this class to virtual webinars, and due to my generosity, tell me I can keep my spot as a gift!

I am amazed. Spirit knew.

June 9, 2016

I don't think my Molly girl will last long. She's very shaky now and has a growth in her neck. I believe Wally knew this and he got the girls here for Dasher. Dasher has never been a solo dog. He has always had Molly with him, and later, Wally.

This is love from Wally, I would say.

June 10, 2016

Dasher is acting very odd. He comes into my office and into my closet and hides behind my clothes. Why are you in there? He sure looks guilty of something. I never did find out what that one was all about!

Molly follows me everywhere lately. Not sure why. Actually, I'm pretending to not know why. Deep down I know her time is coming.

I'm packing supplies for a creative event tomorrow and all of a sudden, I see a quick vision of a lady with brown hair and glasses receiving devastating news. I feel and see how it is shaking her up. I don't recognize the lady. No idea why I received this or who it is about.

Tonight, I shed a lot of tears. I miss you, Wally.

June 11, 2016

I wake with a migraine. Today of all days! It's pouring rain. I pack up and head to my creative event feeling terrible. I want to put my head down and sleep, but I participate in the classes and try to socialize. A lady I've never met before sits next to me. She's really nice. Out of nowhere she receives news that her father has had a heart attack. My stomach drops. *She* was the one in my vision, although I didn't recognize her because she looked different. I feel so terrible for her. I pray for her. She leaves, shaken, just as I had seen in my vision.

I don't know why I was given the vision as I couldn't prevent this tragedy. I find out later that her father – who survived, by the way – had brown hair and glasses. Sometimes these things just get a bit mixed up!

I feel off for the remainder of the event. I have never shared the psychic part of my life with this group of friends, so I keep it to myself. I talk to my family later that evening instead.

It was a very odd day, and I am missing Wally a lot tonight.

June 14, 2016

I've been trying to figure out the reason for that vision. I got it today! I cried a lot for Wally on the night I got the vision. I wanted a sign, a dream, a visit – something! I didn't even associate the vision was from him. I always question if I interpreted Wally's signs and language properly, ever since that dreaded date of March 19 when I agreed to let him go.

Was I right? Did I hear him correctly? Were they his wishes?

Receiving that vision when I asked for a sign was a validation – validation that what he gave me both then and now is accurate. I saw and heard correctly. This vision had nothing to do with me except to prove to myself that I am listening properly to Wally. That is a great comfort to me now. And, it makes the most sense to me about the vision experience itself.

Thank you, Wally.

June 15, 2016

I'm emotional today. Tired of everything. Tired of the pain. I want to sit by the ocean and stare at the sea, nothing else. But I can't go. The ocean is far away and work commitments don't allow me to escape there just yet. I'll be heading there next month. I have to wait.

I get an email. Carmel is doing animal readings. I message her immediately and sign up. Carmel refuses payment and says she's giving me one as a gift. I cry. I tell my son and he cries. It's very touching and thoughtful of her. I can't wait. I'm so thankful.

Wally is definitely finding his way to Carmel! I think this may be what saves my life and my sanity. I hope this will finally heal my pain.

I need to wait for my reading in November but it's something I can look forward to, hold onto and give my Wally the notice to show up. I know he'll show up.

June 19, 2016

I spent some good quality time with Wendy this weekend. She has asked me to go to Jasper with her in July. Her son, Cody, is going to a basketball camp, and she thinks we can go camping nearby while he attends camp. Not sure if I will go or not, but it was nice of her to ask. She thinks it could do me some good to get into the mountains.

June 24, 2016

Wally visited me in my dream! He jumped in front of me – thump – and I got to hug him. I awake so happy. It amazes me when that happens.

I take the dogs out for a walk today. It is all going well until a large jack rabbit crosses our path! The sound that Ryder makes when she sees it is horrific. It reminds me of Wally's voice when he was in so much pain. It mortifies me. It takes me straight back to that terrible time.

Maybe a walk wasn't such a good idea today.

July 7, 2016

Molly hasn't been doing so well over the last few weeks. She hadn't been well since her surgery in February, declining more so lately. I take her to the vet, and he says her liver is failing. There is a yellow tinge in her eyes. I make the difficult decision to let her go and ease her pain in this moment.

Molly passes away in my arms. Tears roll down my face in streams. She was only 12 years old. I tell her I love her, and to say hi to Wally. I'm sure he bulldozed her as she crossed over. He loved doing that when he was alive. He was laughing the whole time doing it too, I swear! Molly likely thought, "Just great – him again!"

I tearfully say as a goodbye, "May you run in the meadows and be pain free and happy, and I'll see you one day!"

I know Molly's better off now. She was so very sick. She didn't bark at the neighbour's dogs any longer. She didn't look out the window at all. She didn't seem to want to do anything any longer.

Having to be in this position again so quickly after losing Wally is extremely tough. Two dogs gone within four months. Too much. Too much pain.

July 20, 2016

I'm hot and have sore feet but I am thoroughly enjoying my summer vacation with my sister. It's been so hectic, and I haven't written a thing! Get ready, here's one big catch up!

It's actually July 26 as I write, but I better start at the beginning. So, I'll begin on July 20, when my mom, sister, niece and I travel to Vancouver, BC.

We get up early and leave early, to arrive at the airport early, and the plane was … early! So, we fly out early and an hour later we are in Vancouver. I call the hotel to see if they have a luggage room we could use because we were … early. Sure thing, so off we go to the hotel. Upon arrival, they inform us that our room is ready … early!

Thank you, Wally!

Everything goes so smoothly. You see, I asked Wally to give us great weather and give us luck and a great trip. We're off to an amazing start. Good boy, Wally! It was raining when we left Edmonton but is sunny in Vancouver – which was a first for them, they say. They had been in a very rainy stretch.

So, again, way to go, Wally!

Our hotel is across from the BC Place venue. We were going to see Adele tonight, and we were all really excited. The Terry Fox statues in his honour are also nearby. Terry Fox was an inspirational young man who raised money for cancer research as he attempted to walk across Canada. It was called the Marathon of Hope. Terry passed away at the age of 22. We settle into our rooms and freshen up and walk to Gastown. We do some shopping there, then head to Canada Place. It's so hot! For lunch we sit at a patio overlooking the harbour and Stanley Park. We had some good laughs, then slowly made our way back to the hotel, stopping to shop and have a coffee break along the way.

As we walk, we come across a basset hound named Rufus. My mom and sister are in Heaven! They love those dogs. It was soon time to go to the Adele concert. We had a fun 1.75 hour wait in line chatting with ladies from Spokane. The time passes quickly as we are all so excited. We enjoy the concert and have such an amazing time.

What a great day!

July 21, 2016

We get up early, have breakfast and leave for Kitsilano Beach. It's my favourite beach in the world. Wally's Spirit is with me as I walk along, beachcombing in my favourite spots. I ask him for a sign that he is here, and sure enough, I find a red heart-shaped stone. I find two more similar red heart-shaped rocks. It is definitely him. I thank him. I walk along with my sister and niece, Brianna, who is trying to find sea glass. She says she wants a large green piece, so I tell her to ask Wally. She does… and you know it! She finds it! It is so funny.

We all enjoy an amazing lunch overlooking the beach. I am so grateful to be sitting with my special family members and with Wally in Spirit. It was truly one of those memories that will last to eternity for me. I had brought a small handful of Wally's ashes with me to scatter along the shore, but in the end, I wasn't sure if I could. Some 'may' have been whisked away in the ocean breeze anyway!

Wally was taking such great care of us on this mini holiday. We finish our stay with a wonderful meal and beautiful scenery as we rotate high above the city.

July 22, 2016

We get up early and head to the airport. It had rained overnight and looked to do so again. Wally had kept us in a beautiful sunshine bubble for our entire stay.

Thank you, Wally.

Today was Wally's birthday. I think about him the entire flight home, wondering why this was the way it had to be. I feel sad and lonely without him. I wish him a happy birthday in Heaven.

My dogs are thrilled to see me when I return, especially Dasher!

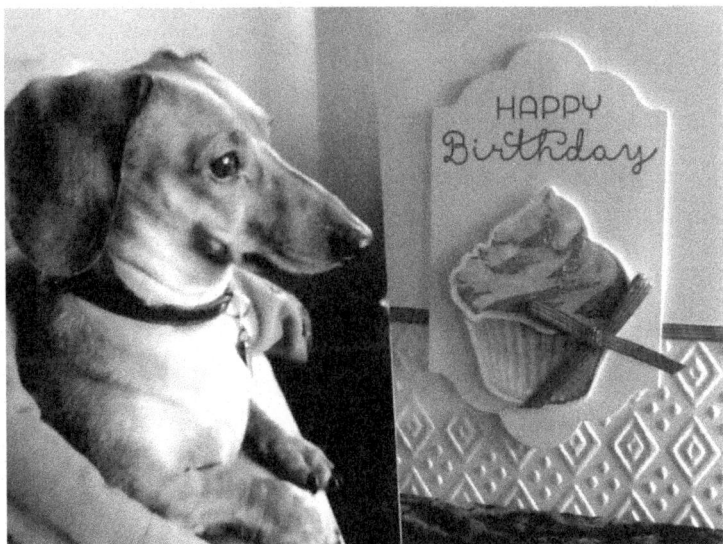

July 23, 2016

What a busy day of laundry and packing! Come home and prepare to leave again. I'm going to Jasper tomorrow. I accepted my sister's invitation to go to the mountains after all. Five days in the mountains will do my soul good.

July 24, 2016

It's 3:30 a.m. and my alarm clock rings. I get up and make sandwiches for our trip. I pack the truck and leave with Dasher at 4:30 a.m. I am not comfortable taking the girls on this trip for some reason, so they are staying behind with Sacha and Randy.

A quick rest stop along the way for Dasher, then I continue northward to my sister's. Dasher and I pass through the town of Whitecourt, and I have a thought about stopping for a coffee. I feel a nudge to continue instead, and I take heed and stay on the road. Shortly out of town, I see something on the road in the distance. It's a mama duck and about ten babies trying to cross the busy highway. I brake hard. The vehicle behind me changes lanes to overtake and doesn't see the ducks. I open my window and wave frantically. Luckily, they stop.

The ducks turn around and head back to the ditch and the trees.

Spirit directed that nudge for sure! I catch my breath and continue on.

After three hours, I arrive at my sister's. I transfer my luggage and Dasher to her motorhome. At 9 a.m. we depart. My sister, nephew, myself, and four dogs in total! One of her dogs really wanted to go, so he was added in at the last minute. Quite the caravan load! Wally would have loved this! An adventure with friends – what could be better?

We arrive in Jasper after 2 p.m. and proceed directly to the school where my nephew registers for the basketball camp, then we register and set up at our campground at Whistler's Campground, just a few kilometres out of the Jasper townsite. We are warned about two grizzly bears that had been spotted nearby. I am grateful the girls stayed home. We set up a large kennel fence and put our lawn chairs within that perimeter. If we had to make a run for it, we could easily get inside fast! All of us!

We sat in our chairs in our kennel, and Dasher began to growl. We don't see anything, at first, until a group of elk appear from behind us. Munching grass and not caring about us, they wander through and away.

Good job, Dasher! Great watchdog!

July 25, 2016

What an amazing sleep I had last night. The mountain air is amazing! After dropping Cody at his camp, Wendy and I take a short drive to Edith Lake to spend a few hours enjoying the beauty and the lake itself. It is a beautiful spot. Quiet, peaceful, calm, and scenic. The dogs stay in the motorhome as I help Wendy carry the kayak down to the lake. Wendy and her cocker spaniel, Rascal, go kayaking. I walk alone for a bit. As I walk, I see Pyramid Mountain to my left in the distance, looking spectacular. It's my favourite mountain. I snap some great photos.

A bird flies by me, and hovers. It looks like it is checking out what I am doing. "Hi Wally," I say, laughing. It's a type of woodpecker. On the walk back, I ask Wally to show me something spectacular. Immediately I find a piece of bark shaped exactly like a bird. Unbelievable. Of course, I take a picture as proof. Perfect. Spectacular!

I return to the motorhome to doggie welcomes and wags! We wait for Wendy to text me when she's finished so I can help her carry the kayak back. Time flies and before I know it we're back in the townsite of Jasper. We parked outside the school to wait for Cody. Wendy sits next to me. A brown bird hops along the grass and comes right over. The bird stands there looking at us.

Wendy says, "Is that Wally?"

"Yup," I say, and we both laugh.

Today is also the anniversary of my dad's passing. I know he is with my sister and I today as well.

Thank you for the special bird bark moment today, Wally.

July 26, 2016

To say I love rocks and crystals is an understatement – I love them! After making a purchase at a crystal shop in Jasper, I notice the design on the store's bag was a cartoon rock dachshund. I smile. I smile even more as I return to the campsite and look at my finds. I had bought some crystals and a new set of oracle cards. The oracle cards had beautiful peacock artwork.

The artwork on the cards is by Josephine Wall. I hadn't noticed this in the shop! I love her work and own many of her calendars. It's beautiful – pictures within pictures. The more you look at it, the more you see something you didn't see before. It reminds me of life's journey.

Later that day, there were more peacocks. Wally strikes again!

I'd always wanted the perfect dream catcher. On the next shopping trip later today, I find it. The dreamcatcher has a beautiful peacock feather in it. Of course it does.

Thank you, Wally.

July 27, 2016

Once again Wendy and I decide to do a short drive out of Jasper after dropping Cody at his basketball camp. This time we stop at a spot off the highway and walk down to the river. It is really high and fast flowing. My sister has a bad feeling about the place – thinks a bear is nearby. We load up the dogs quickly and leave. I always tell her to listen to her intuition. We find out later that a grizzly bear was seen in that area that day.

We visit the tourist information booth in Jasper later in the day. I stand in one spot and hear cooing sounds. Sure enough, above me is a pigeon.

Ahh, a lot of noticeable signs all vacation long from Wally. Him and his feather signs!

July 28, 2016

While shopping in Jasper today, a cashier told me how they had five weeks of rain until the day we arrived. It was hot and sunny while we stayed. I felt like telling him that Wally did it for me and how the rain would return when we left …

July 29, 2016

Basketball camp has finished. Wendy, Cody and I go sightseeing. Pyramid Mountain is our first destination. The colours are amazing. Pinks and oranges and glints of fool's gold make it one spectacular mountain to look at. We park and all of us, including the dogs, walk down the boardwalk. It takes us to a small island on Pyramid Lake. From there the view of Pyramid Mountain is even more spectacular as it's unobstructed. The mountain is massive and magnificent.

Our next stop is at a riding stable. Wendy and Cody go horseback riding while I wait with the dogs.

I take lots of pictures. One of the remaining horses is standing in his pen looking at me. I mean, *really* looking at me. I know it was Wally doing this. The horse has the same colouring as Wally as well as his "look". I take his picture. When my sister and nephew return, the horse goes about his business eating as if nothing happened.

It is truly such a wonderful day. I reflect on my dad off and on this day. It was the anniversary of his funeral. In the afternoon, we sit around the campsite and as I look up, I see a heart in the clouds. I take a picture.

I love you, Wally.

July 30, 2016

It's departure day! The end of the Jasper trip. Just as I thought they would, the rains come as we leave. We arrive at my sister's late afternoon, and I head home almost immediately. When Dasher and I stop for fuel, a bird comes up to me.

Hi, Wally!

A second bird with a dead dragonfly in its mouth comes to me as well. They both stay nearby for a bit and then fly off. I finish fuelling and am going to leave but a train is approaching, closing the highway so I wait. All of a sudden, one of the two birds jumps on the hood of my truck! Startled, I say, "Yes, I see you, Wally!"

As I drive, I realize I had felt sad about Wally since I entered Whitecourt, the town about an hour from my sister's home. The bird encounter lifts my Spirits.

I laugh again, thinking of the dragonfly. Ever since Molly passed, whenever I sit outside at home, a dragonfly often flies and hovers near me. It feels like a feminine energy and I think of Molly immediately. I always say "Hi Molly" when the dragonfly appears.

Wally wanted to validate Molly being the 'dragonfly'.

July 31, 2016

I have had such a great vacation. Between Vancouver and Jasper, and all that time with my family, it has really strengthened my relationship with my sister and my Wally on the other side.

For both, I am very grateful.

August 13, 2016

When I speak to my mom on the phone, something doesn't seem right. As the day goes on, I continue to get nudges to call her again. I hear the message, "Her meds aren't right." I call her back and tell her to go through her medicine with me. Instead of antibiotics she had been given anti-anxiety meds – and a big dose! The pharmacy has made an error. No wonder she doesn't sound right.

Thank you, Spirit, for pushing me on this one to sort things out.

August 19, 2016

Nearly five months ago My Little Wally became Spirit once more. The devastating heartbreak nearly broke my own Spirit completely. I have never had such a profound loss. Thankfully, my spiritual work, classes, and meditation all helped me understand and connect to Wally. I am very grateful for this continuing relationship with him, and I know it will continue to get stronger and stronger. Wally and I are bonded with our love for eternity, and I know that without a doubt.

I adored Wally then.

I adore him now.

I love you, Wally.

August 21, 2016

It's Sunday morning and there's a lot of squawking going on outside my window on the deck. I look out. There sits a large magpie next to the loveseat, squawking loudly to get my attention. He's pecking at a rawhide bone! Seriously! Hi Wally! The magpie carries it to the lawn, then flies on top of the playhouse. So funny.

Yes, I see you, Wally!

September 5, 2016

After dinner I walk to our local library to check out some new books. On my way back, at a specific section near the mall, I ask Wally to show me a sign that he is with me. "Make it a really clear sign for me, Wally," I say. I walk around the corner and come upon the green space. There are well over 100 birds sitting there! Ravens make up the majority with a few seagulls.

Thanks Wally! This was a good one! Birds – feathers! Always birds and feathers. That's our thing. The funny part is that I walked through this exact greenspace on my way to the library ten minutes prior and there were only two ravens in a tree.

As I walk by, the birds sat there, unafraid and not moving. I take a photo on my phone but it doesn't work, oddly enough.

September 10, 2016

I am volunteering at the Ranch for their fair. I enjoy being there. I'm outdoors looking at trees and leaves, and it's simply the best. The Ranch has an energy to it unlike anywhere I know. It's beautiful.

As I walk to my truck later that evening when the festivities end, I feel a bit sad. I hadn't seen Walter the Peacock all day. I get in my truck, start it up and look forward. Directly in front of me, sitting on the hood of a truck is Walter the Peacock. He is looking directly at me. I take two photos. Walter jumps onto the top of the truck's cab. Yes, I see you, Walter! I am so thrilled.

Thank you, Walter.

This is so soothing to my heart. I have to wait for a long train to finish crossing my road on my way home which allows me time to relax and let the day's events sink in.

Beautiful. Thank you, Wally.

Part 4

Trusting Spirit

September 11, 2016

As I drive to the Ranch this morning, I ask Wally to show himself again. I park, look to my left and there is Walter the Peacock on the same truck! As I walk toward the house, I hear him squawk and turn to look. My heart lifts. "I see you, Wally." It was so awesome. It turns out to be a very chilly day working outside, but I share many laughs with my fellow volunteers. As the day goes on, I feel like I am getting a sore throat or a cold.

This night is an unusual night. I stay awake all night long. Spirit keeps at me all night to tell upper management at work a few things. I write notes and notes and try to go to sleep, but there is more! Challenge them, they say. You don't want to change jobs.

I had been directed to take a position that was the same level I had held 15 years ago! I didn't want to move backwards. All due to restructuring plans.

The final message says, "Do it now before their day begins." It is 4 a.m.

I email my challenge, and it gets their attention.

September 12, 2016

It takes them until this evening to respond. I am very disappointed, to say the least. I know right then that I don't want to stay. What to do? I feel trapped.

Spirit gives me subtle hints; tells me I have enough vacation pay to last two weeks and that I have savings that could buy me time to find something else.

September 15, 2016

I listen to Spirit and resign. It is the Full Moon – Harvest Moon – so a great day to release! I give them their required two weeks' notice.

September 16, 2016

I discover an ad in the local newspaper. One day after my job finishes, free at our community centre, there was going to be an all-day event featuring local authors and illustrators and publishers!

Now I know I had made the right decision.

September 30, 2016

Today is my last day of work. It's been a tough two weeks, but I have maintained my personal mandate of being kind. In these last weeks, I have gone above expectations in training others. They all thanked me and wished I was staying, and wished me well, which was nice. There have been lots of supporting signs throughout my final two weeks that I was doing the right thing at the right time.

When I drop off my computer and office equipment, I am free.

Spirit has told me this must happen. They have said that my books need to get into the world – the world is ready for Wally! I'm excited and somewhat apprehensive for this chapter to begin.

I take my son to the pool then go for a walk.

Wally, we're going to be okay, I say.

I walk a few steps more and a raven begins chattering at me from a tree branch above. I walk a few more steps and a white feather crosses my path. I take a picture of it. I feel complete comfort and confident that all is well. I am proud of myself for being courageous enough to take a leap of faith and listen to my intuition and messages from Spirit.

I have no regrets. I look forward to what life and Spirit have in store for me – and for Wally.

October 1, 2016

Free to do what I want today, I attend the Words in the Park event. I learn a lot and meet some amazing people. It feels so right.

November 15, 2016

Today is my reading with Carmel Joy Baird. I'm excited and anxious both. Carmel starts by passing on a message from my Dad. He says, "There's a dog here chomping at the bit to talk to you but I'm going first!" We both laugh. Other personal messages come through that bring much comfort and validation. My Dad says he is taking care of Wally, that he's sitting on his knee right now. His tail is wagging in happy excitement. Wally likes the fact his ashes are home. Wally says, "No sweaters are needed in Heaven."

"The lesson in losing Wally is all about growth, releasing, finding yourself and connecting yourself with your Spirit," Carmel says. "Peacock is your animal spirit at this time. Blues, greens, and gold are key colours for you. Wally says it is okay for the dogs to share his toys and bed but not his collar. Wally says he misses your sister Wendy. He loves her. Even now where the sunbeams hit the floor, Wally lies there. He pushes Ryder out of the way sometimes. Wally laughs as he is saying this."

Carmel tells me that I understood Wally like no one ever had before. He was like the heart and soul of you. Wally was focussed on you. He wanted to be everything to you. He was a part of your soul family, and that he finds you in every lifetime. Wally is a very old soul.

Carmel tells me that Wally communicated with me through his eyes. "You understand that?" she asks.

"Yes, very much so," I reply.

Carmel spoke a bit about Molly as well. "Molly is really healthy now. She had been sick for some time. It was her time to go, and she was thankful to go. Wally was especially thankful to go as well. Molly was close to you but not the same way as Wally. She's still connected by spirit and in the home a lot too."

I thank Carmel for the reading and say goodbye. I sit there thinking about everything. I jot down notes as quickly as I can to remember the key messages. I feel relieved and comforted and am glad to have had both my Dad and Wally come through like that.

November, 2016

The rest of November I spend my extra time writing and taking classes, reading, napping and soul searching.

I continue to grieve.

I still miss My Little Wally.

December, 2016

Nearing Christmas, I really want something to take my mind off missing Wally so much. Be careful what you wish for, I find out! I have the most bizarre experience with a mystery rash from my artificial Christmas tree. My arm looks very angry, and I end up in emergency getting intravenous antibiotics on Christmas Day. I have to go home with the intravenous needle still inserted as I will need more sessions in the coming days to conquer the mystery bacteria.

I really do get something to take my mind off grieving for a bit.

As luck would have it, I end up having the mystery rash reappear three times in total over the next few months. I have to go on intravenous drugs each time. In February, the bacteria battle ends. I am grateful to move forward.

February 5, 2017

Today I attend a meditation course. I know a few people in attendance, but one friend, Vanessa, in particular catches my eye as she is wearing a magnificent pair of peacock leggings! I compliment her on them and she tells me a story. While getting ready that morning, while she was taking a hanger from her closet, the pair of leggings flew out!

"Without a lie they flew!" she says. She hadn't worn them in a while so thought why not.

We both smile. Wally was there too!

February 6, 2017

I'm feeling anxious today for some reason. Maybe I'm missing Wally. It's a cold day too. In the car, I notice the licence plate of a vehicle ahead: WALLYBE, it reads.

This is comforting. Everything will be okay.

Thanks, Wally!

February 23, 2017

I look at my calendar for today and see an image of an owl next to some writing and dismiss it.

As the day goes on, I ask Wally for a sign to cheer me up.

When I look at my calendar again that evening, I laugh. It isn't an owl! Even though I swear I saw an owl earlier, it is, in fact, a peacock!

Thank you, Wally, yet again!

February 27, 2017

I attend class tonight at the Ranch and ask Wally to show up. Sure enough, Walter the Peacock is on top of the fence. We look at each other as I drive by, and I say, "Hi Wally!"

Love it when that happens!

March 2, 2017

Today I read through my journal. I read from a year ago, about Wally's death. It brings back all the very raw emotion. I sob as it takes me back. I read it now to get it over with instead of waiting for and dreading March 19. My eyes burn from the tears. Sad tears hurt more than happy tears.

I'm glad I journaled the memories and emotions, heartbreaking as they are. I'm glad I documented them.

March 19, 2017

Exactly one year ago to the date, you crossed the Rainbow Bridge, Wally. What a time. What a year. What a loss. My heart was put through the shredder, leaving me to pick up all the pieces and put it back together somehow.

It amazes me how Spirit brings special messages when needed.

Today I receive a picture of a dachshund that looks exactly like Wally. It is wearing a peacock costume! How I laugh. How perfect for today.

April 1, 2017

I attend another creative event. A lady hears me speak about my dachshunds and asks me about their colouring. She offers up a story about her grandson's dachshund and shows me a photo of him. He is the same as Wally! The same colouring. She tells me his name is Walter. I tell her about my Wally a tiny bit.

Thank you for orchestrating such a specific message, Wally!

April 3, 2017

My son tells me about a substitute teacher he had that day. "Guess what his name was, Mom? His name is Mr. Peacock!"

I love the fact that my son recognizes signs as well.

May 12, 2017

All day I felt blue. I miss Wally. I'm a bit apprehensive about visiting the pet medium Brianna. There are a few of us here, I hope I don't have to wait long. Brianna will draw names to decide the order of readings.

Fortunately, my name is drawn first. I'm so relieved. I pass Wally's photo to Brianna, and she tells me how Wally is so thankful that I was the last one he saw before he passed away. She tells me that Wally could communicate with me through his eyes, just like Carmel did. Everyone in this intimate group is crying, including myself.

She goes on to say that he plays jokes on the dogs, pinches them and moves their toys. He loves to sunbathe.

"Did he like to dig?" she asks.

I tell her about the special digging tree.

"Did you put his ashes there?"

I say I did.

"It's okay for the other dogs to go to that tree. Let them smell his collar."

She goes on to ask me if I had changed his name. I laugh. Yes, I had changed the spelling of his name. He came as Walle but I changed it to Wally. This wasn't common knowledge! She also asks me if I had thought about getting him stuffed, which I had. I considered submitting his photo to a company that would build a stuffy of him. No one except Wally knew that!

Brianna tells me that I had nightmares about his passing and that his death was so traumatic to me. She tells me to keep the photo I had handed her. She says, "It's him looking right into your eyes! Don't lose it!"

It was really amazing and felt like a conversation directly with Wally.

The night brought me such peace.

July 22, 2017

It's Wally's birthday today. I pack to head to my sister's. We are returning to Jasper for another basketball camp for my nephew, Cody. I stop at the bank and then a local café. As I stand in line, I keep hearing Wally say, "Take Dasher for safety". It repeats over and over. Finally, I say, "Okay" and return home and collect Dasher and pack his things.

I tell my sister the story when I arrive at her home

I'm not sure if I needed Dasher for the drive, or if I needed him for our upcoming Jasper trip, but I listened and took him with me. There never seemed to be any actual danger, but I enjoyed having Dasher with me.

July 23, 2017

We pull into our camping spot and set up, already enjoying the lovely mountain air.

July 24, 2017

My niece, Brianna, has joined us for a few days on this trip. She and I go shopping for a few hours. When we return, my sister has an amazing story to share.

She had taken the dogs for a long walk. On her journey around the campsite, she heard a lady calling, "Wally" in the distance.

"Who are you looking for?" my sister asked. "I'll keep an eye out."

"My mom and my dog Wally. My mom gets a bit disoriented in the campsite," she said. "Wally is a dachshund."

Even before hearing that detail, my sister knew it, because of the feeling she had while hearing Wally called in the woods. As my sister relayed the story a huge smile grew across my face with such love in my heart.

Wally is here and we all feel the significance.

February 15, 2018

It takes me a while after I wake up to realize the meaning of last night's Wally dream. Wally visited – on Valentine's Day! That's why he showed up. It was his way to show his love too.

I miss him and love him.

March 3, 2018

I've been reading a lot about writing a book lately. I've listened to some online webinars about the same. Today, I finally came up with my book title which is something I've been struggling with for a long time.

I am excited about this inspiration.

April 6, 2018

Today I drive to a nearby city. I am going to attend a creative event tomorrow. I arrive early and check in at the hotel. I take a drive after that to find the conference location and do a bit of shopping. I find a peacock journal and a dachshund journal. Perfect.

I return to the hotel and organize all my journals and write and write and write. I manage to get through some of my most difficult pages and six hours later I am mentally exhausted.

April 7, 2018

I enjoy all the learnings at the conference and am creatively exhausted by day's end. I eat supper and turn in early for the night.

April 8, 2018

Check out time is noon today. I still have a few hours to finish up what I can. When I open the curtains, I see snow has fallen. My gaze is drawn to a pattern on a cement barrier below. From this height, it looks like a line of dachshunds walking through the snow. Incredible.

Did that lift me up? You bet it did!

June 1, 2018

Last night's dream was very different. I dreamt that Peacock Walter jumped on my knee like a dog, and that I pet him like a dog. I stroked his gorgeous feathers as if they were fur.

It definitely made me happy.

July 24, 2018

I had a job interview today with a new department. I think it went well.

July 25, 2018

Dasher isn't feeling well. Vet says he has diabetes and pancreatitis. He needs insulin twice a day and his diet must change. Randy, Sacha and I learn how to do the insulin injections even though we all have anxiety doing them.

August 14, 2018

I can tell Dasher isn't feeling well today. I call his vet but she says she doesn't have time to deal with him today even though I think it's serious. What?! That angers me considering how long I've been going there.

Randy and I drive to the vet hospital instead, the same one I took Wally to. Already we're both anxious. Randy says Dasher has a smell to him. I can't smell anything unusual. Vet says Dasher is dehydrated and needs his ketone levels checked. This can go two ways she warns: one good, one devastating. The vet tests him and we wait for results.

The results are good! They will help him, but he'll likely remain in hospital for a few days. Dasher is admitted. The vet tells us that Randy could smell the ketones in Dasher. Some people can smell them, others not.

"How odd," I think.

August 15, 2018

Great news this morning! Dasher had a good night and is now standing and alert. His ketones will be measured again today. Randy and I visit. He looks so much better! His eyes are a bit glazed, but overall he looks so much better. I feel a great relief. Dasher may be able to come home tomorrow if tonight goes well. I love seeing him so well. Quite the positive change from yesterday.

August 16, 2018

I call the vet. Dasher had a good night but four units of insulin isn't working on the blood sugars. The vet will try alternate numbers today to bring the sugars down. I think Dasher will be released tomorrow instead. I continue to pray that diet can fix his pancreas and then he'll totally never need insulin ever again! Oh, how that would be so nice. I feel very tired and drained today with my worry for Dasher.

August 17, 2018

The vet calls and tells me Dasher's insulin dosage is still weird. I go to visit Dasher after work by myself. Instead of a visit, I get news that he can come home with me! I am so happy! I'm finishing the paperwork and payment and Dasher comes running out of the back. I kneel to grab him as he has no collar on. He jumps on me, kissing me all over, knocking me down onto the floor, lying flat. I was laughing and he was still kissing me. Other pet owners waiting in that room were laughing too. Dasher was celebrating freedom and me! It was wonderful.

I surprised Randy and Sacha with our homecoming. Tonight was a happy, joyful night.

August 22, 2018

Today is my first day at my new job. I'm thankful they have many dog lovers here as I explain a bit about Dasher's situation. They understand what I'm going through.

August 24, 2018

Dasher looks sick today. He's very lethargic. I can't give him his insulin as he hasn't eaten enough yet. I'm worried.

August 25, 2018

Today I take Dasher to a new vet, closer to my home. I am really impressed with the caring attitude of everyone I speak with. The vet adjusts Dasher's insulin. We'll see how he does. The vet also gives me his home phone number in case of emergency.

That was so kind and unexpected.

September 8, 2018

Dasher is having a seizure! He's making odd noises and body movements. I call the vet to tell him we're on our way in. My heart is racing at this point. Upon arrival, the vet starts an intravenous drip and Dasher comes out of his seizure. His blood is tested, and his blood sugars are really off. The vet gives him an injection and we head home nervously.

September 10, 2018

I stay home from work with a migraine, which ends up as a real blessing. I spend the day cuddling and hugging Dasher and crying. Huge tears. I'm noticing he has tremors – he isn't himself. He doesn't respond to me in his usual way, doesn't nudge my hand to pet him. He doesn't give me kisses. The Dasher I know is gone. It is so hard to think about letting him go.

Dasher refuses to eat and drink despite my emotional pleas. Please Dasher, please Dasher, I cry. Fortunately, Sacha is at school and not witnessing this. Randy's at work. I'm alone with Dasher and holding his paw in my hand, pleading with him to try to hold on and eat and drink something.

Years ago, I sat with a basketful of puppies. I was to choose the puppy I wanted. Instead, Dasher made his way to the top of the basket to choose me.

"Okay buddy, I see you want to come with me. Let's go!" I said.

Dasher was the size of a pound of butter. He was the smallest of the litter and had a big scratch across his forehead. I was more than delighted he chose me.

I was there at that beginning, and I was going to be there when he passed away.

September 11, 2018

Dasher passes away in my arms today at the vet's office. I stay with him, until the end.

He was so sick and had been declining rapidly in the previous days. Refusing to eat and drink and developing ticks and tremors and having mini seizures, I knew … and my heart broke.

I loved Dasher like a baby. He was wonderful. He was my body-guard on road trips. He was my camping buddy. He was my rock that helped me through the dark days of grief after Wally died. He took care of me. I prayed to save him but it wasn't meant to be.

A few hours after Dasher passes, I sit outside crying and looking up to the sky. I notice a cloud. It looks like a smiling, running Wally and to his right, I see Molly's face, and sure enough to the above right of her, Dasher! He has crossed over and let me know he is okay, and that they are all together.

Thank you!

I'm sure there was quite the celebration when Dasher was greeted by Wally and Molly. Molly likely says, "Thank goodness you're here! Wally's been driving me crazy!"

Dasher was never alone. He came to us when we had Molly, then he had Reese and Ryder. In crossing over, Wally and Molly welcomed him. He was never alone there either. I am truly grateful for that. Having lost both boys now is very difficult as the energy has changed again in my home.

My heart is so cracked I feel that I could simply crumble in any given moment. Sacha is devastated. He grew up with Dasher. They held a special bond. Sacha named Dasher the moment I chose him and from that day forward, Dasher thought Sacha was his baby and was so protective of Sacha. If I or anyone tried to hug Sacha, Dasher would come barking to ensure his Sacha was okay. It always made us laugh.

September 12, 2018

It's now 24 hours since losing Dasher and waves of grief come and go. I never know when or what will set me off. Care and compassion of others brings more tears. I miss my little Dasher so very much, all his quirks and voice and actions. I'm grateful I have video and photos of him. I think of the pure softness of his ears – those big Batman ears! How I loved to caress those ears.

He truly was such a cute boy. So sweet. Incredibly sweet.

The fond memories I have of him help ease the pain. The first snow is happening, and I am grateful Dasher isn't dealing with the cold weather today.

September 13, 2018

I'm sad at work today. It's quiet and my mind is constantly think-ing of Dasher. The vet office calls me to say Dasher's ashes are ready. I'm not ready! I assumed they would be in the following week. Ashes make it all so final.

It's snowing again and I feel as dreary as the weather.

I miss you, Dasher.

September 25, 2018

Today is the two-week anniversary of losing Dasher. My boss brings me a magpie feather. If only he knew what that means to me. He has no idea of the significance of yet another feather!

October 8, 2018

It's Thanksgiving and I'm melancholy with the accumulated loss-es of my dogs. In the kitchen, I experience an amazing Dasher moment. I suddenly feel a dog behind my legs, I feel the fur. I look and there is no dog. I know it is Dasher. He always hid behind my legs if he heard a loud noise.

October 11, 2018

Today I am in a course for work. I ask Dasher for a sign. I have to say, both he and Wally deliver bigtime! One slide in the presenta-tion was of a peacock – there's Wally! Not long after, there is a slide of a little dog that reminds me of Dasher, with his ears up and his shadow on the ground with the saying, "Holy Crap, I'm Batman!" Batman, of course.

I love my boys in Heaven!

Thank you, Dasher and Wally.

October 20, 2018

I am shopping today and ask the boys for a sign to make me feel better. The boys tend to send more signs than Molly. I think it's because I always had a strong connection with them while Molly was more attached to Randy. Randy fondly called her Mollygirl.

At one store, I find three perfect dachshund Christmas cannisters tucked away on a low shelf. At another store, I find a wooden stamp (stamping is a favourite hobby) that has dog faces in the shape of a Christmas tree, with Dasher as the star! I love it! At checkout as I wait, I notice a stuffed animal with two big eyes and two big ears staring at me. I pull it out of the pile. It's a purple Dasher with big Batman ears!

Yes, I bought it all.

Thanks, boys.

January 1, 2019

Happy New Year! It's quiet around here except for the sound of the washing machine right now. I see the crescent shape of the moon and one glowing star as I look out my window. Clouds are low and dark, then there's a stretch of clear sky above that. The sun should rise soon. A cool wind gently nudges the tree branches, but it's warmed up from last night.

Taking advantage of the quiet morning, I work on writing projects. I also try an abstract ink technique I had read about that caught my interest. Holding my breath, I carefully pull my papers apart to reveal the random pattern results of the technique. Well, I cannot believe my eyes. The colours are perfect, and the design is a Divine creation. The pattern is that of an abstract dachshund! That's what I see in it and I am excited beyond words!

I feel elated. I look forward to this new year of possibilities. I have so much to be grateful for, and don't have to chase the future constantly. It will come. I have a wonderful son who has the most beautiful smile and I try to make him smile often so I can look at it!

My two mini dachshunds are wonderful healers. I'm grateful for them.

Author's Note

Onwards

As time goes on, my heartache lessens a bit more each day. It has taken me nearly two years to be able to talk about Wally's death without crying or having my voice crack and tremble, except when I read the first few pages of this book that is. Time wasn't healing the wounds; it was merely changing my reactions to the wounds.

Anyone who says it's easy or not emotional to write a book didn't write mine! It was a painful journey writing my story and countless times I thought of giving up as it hurt so much to relive the heartaches.

Readings, healings, prayers, the outdoors and meditations have all been beneficial to me in my healing journey. I love to journal, and my journals helped me almost as much as the signs from Wally. I was able to safely capture my personal feelings and I captured many memories of Wally. My dogs were also key in my healing making me laugh and keeping me company.

Last night I saw a great example of this. As I was lying on the loveseat, both Reese and Ryder decided I needed company right then! Ryder pulled herself into positions that were definitely directed by Wally and Dasher both. I laughed at both dogs competing for the right positions next to me.

Then it hit me. I was laughing. I was laughing with Reese and Ryder and Wally and Dasher. I will be okay. I feel my ashes pendant and it's warm to the touch from my body.

Thank you, Wally, you saved me many times.

About the Author

C.J. Protz is a spiritual intuitive empath who tries to bring kindness and laughter to those who share her path. C.J. loves animals – especially dachshunds and peacocks!

C.J. enjoys writing, camping, stamping, crafting, rock hunting, beachcombing, reading, learning and laughing. She shares her home in Sherwood Park, Alberta, Canada with her two beautiful mini dachshunds who provide many comical moments of joy and laughter!

And of course, C.J. loves talking to Wally – every day.

Photos of Wally and some items mentioned in this book can be found at www.cjprotz.com